My First Plane Trip

KIM JENKINS

Authors note

Most of the books on this subject use cartoons or graphics to help children learn about air travel. I decided to present the content with real photos to walk your child through the experience of taking an airplane trip. If your son or daughter is even just a bit nervous about flying, this book will help to chase the butterflies away.

Packing for your trip

Before you can leave for your trip you have to take some time to pack important items like clothing, toys, books, and your favorite stuffed animal. Your parents can help you write a list of what to bring and check your suitcase when you have gathered everything.

Do you have butterflies?

If this is your first time on a plane you might get butterflies in your tummy. These aren't real butterflies but maybe you feel a bit scared or nervous about the big trip. Everyone gets a bit nervous when they try something new for the first time, even your parents. Try listening to calming music, drawing a picture, or just snuggling with a parent. Those butterflies will fly away in no time.

You should probably leave Mr. Pebbles at home since he doesn't appear to be in a flying mood today.

Going to the airport

You may have to get up really early in the morning and it might still be dark outside. If your flight is in the morning you have to get there early to make sure you get to your plane on time. Your parents might drive their car or maybe they will hire a taxi cab or a limousine to take you to the airport. I like the limousine idea.

When you get to the airport keep an eye out for the control tower. The tower is a very tall building. This is where the air traffic controllers work. They make sure all the planes take off and land at the right time.

Image courtesy of B

Check out this control tower! The crazy building in front is a restaurant, if you visit this airport, in Los Angeles, California, maybe you can have lunch there. The building in the background is the control tower.

Check-in

When you arrive at the airport you can give your suitcases to the airline and print off your tickets. Your Mom or Dad may have printed the tickets at home or if they have a smartphone they may have your tickets right on their phone.

Look around for the flight board you can find your flight on the board to see what time it leaves.

✈ DEPARTURES			
Time	Flight	Destination	Gate
12:00	OD 1961	TORONTO	06
12:15	PN 0034	VANCOUVER	18
12:20	T3 0529	MONTREAL	32
12:30	PN 2415	CALGARY	14
12:50	GI 1872	OTTAWA	09
12:55	T3 0944	HALIFAX	27
13:20	SF 2778	EDMONTON	20
13:45	OD 0061	WINNIPEG	31
13:50	BK 1532	YELLOWKNIFE	04
14:05	OD 3487	VICTORIA	12
14:30	PN 0194	REGINA	03
14:35	SF 0028	SASKATOON	08

The airline will weigh your bags to make sure they are not too heavy. After they weigh your suitcases they will put labels on them to tell the baggage handlers where to send your bags. Your suitcases will be put in the cargo area underneath your plane and will fly with you.

Head to the gate

You will have to go through the security area first.

They may ask your parents to take off their shoes and jackets to go through an XRAY machine. No worries, the XRAY is safe, it allows the airline to make sure you aren't taking on anything that is against the rules. For example, you shouldn't bring a **porcupine** with you, they might not allow that through security.

Some airports have really cool tunnels to go out to the gates. This tunnel is in Chicago O'Hare airport. Many flights will stop in Chicago on the way across the United States.

Other airports use buses to move people around the terminals. This is a great chance to see the airplanes up close as the bus takes you around the tarmac to your gate.

Time to Shop

Once you get through security, you can relax at your gate and wait for your plane to board. They have lots of gift and snack shops by the gates. If you arrive early and have some extra time your parents may even buy you something special. Or you can buy a gift for someone you are going to visit or someone you miss who did not get to go on the trip with you.

JUST NO PORCUPINES

Boarding Time

The airline staff will announce when it is time to board the plane. They usually let people with young children on the plane first so listen for that announcement. Take a look at your ticket and it will tell you what seat number you have. The number will tell you the row you are in and the letter tells you if your seat is by the window or the aisle.

When you board you should try to get to your seat as quickly as you can so everyone can get on board. When you first enter to the plane, look to your left, you may get a chance to see the cockpit and maybe the pilot. Sometimes if you ask and they have some extra time, the pilots will even talk with you about how they fly the plane.

Preparing for Takeoff

The flight attendants will show you all of the safety features of the airplane and then they will come by to make sure your seat belt is fastened, you may have to turn off your electronic devices for takeoff or they may let you keep them turned on, it depends on the airline.

Don't worry; you can turn them on again when you hear three bells go off about 10 minutes after takeoff. Before you take off your plane will probably have to wait in line on the tarmac, also called the runway. At busy airports this can take a while. When the plane is ready to take off the captain will make an announcement to ask the flight attendants to take their seat. The plane may make some strange noises as it is getting ready to take off, it is normal, it is just the plane's systems getting ready for takeoff.

Some planes have TV's on them so you can watch your favorite shows while you fly.

Up, Up, and Away

Sometimes the first few minutes of flight can be a bit bumpy, but it is nothing to worry about. Just like when you are riding in your car and you feel some bumps in the road there are bumps in the air too. Once the pilot gets the flight up to its cruising altitude it will be smooth sailing. After you hear those three bells many things will happen.

My First Plane Trip

The captain will turn off the fasten seat belt sign which means you can get up and go to the bathroom if you need to.

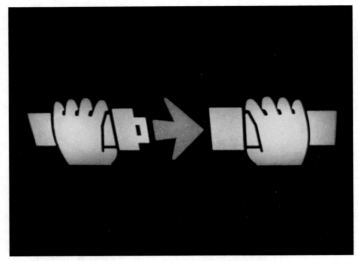

They always have at least one bathroom on each plane. Then flight attendants will come down the aisle offering free drinks like juice, water, and coffee for the grown-ups. Sit back and enjoy the flight.

Time to Land

About 20 minutes before landing, the pilot will announce his plans to land the plane. You might feel some pressure in your ears as the plane descends. Try chewing on a piece of gum or candy, if you don't have anything, you can just pretend to swallow that will release the pressure in your ears.

You may have to turn off your electronic devices, make sure your seat belt is fastened. By the way, you should always keep your seat belt fastened when you are seated just in case there are a few bumps in the air. When you hear the landing gear come down, you know you are close to landing.

Image courtesy of Benson Kua @ Flickr

This is a great time to look out the window and see the city or town that you will be visiting.

Don't forget your suitcase

If you carried your suitcase on the plane (small bags only), then you just need to take them with you.

If you checked in your suitcase back when you were getting your tickets, then you have to walk down to the baggage claim area and pick up your bags. They will appear on a carrousel that goes around and around.

Now that you read this book you will know more about flying than most of the people on your plane. Looks like Mr. Pebbles feels much better about flying too and wants to bring along a friend.

Here are a few things you can bring with you:

1) Deck of cards
2) Puzzle book
3) Your favorite doll or action figure
4) A notebook or coloring book and some crayons or pencils
5) Some snacks but no drinks or liquids until after you go through security
6) Chewing gum or Life Savers just in case you need to pop your ears.

REMEMBER, no porcupines on the plane!

Questions and Answers

Can planes fly when it is raining?

Yes they can fly in rain or snow, but if there is a thunder and lightning storm the pilot will wait under the storm finishes before taking off.

Can I sit together with my family?

When your parents booked the flight, they had the option to select their seats, hopefully they found seats next to each other. If your seats are not together, don't worry about it, they can usually take care of it when you get to the airport.

Can I sit next to the window?

Sure you can, just ask your parents to pick a seat next to the window for you when they book the flight. If you are under 16 you can't sit in an Exit Row. These are special rows that have a door to exit the plane if needed.

Can I plug in my electronic gadgets?

Only a few airlines offer power while in flight so make sure to charge up your device before you go.

People You Might Meet

Baggage Clerk: When you arrive at the airport, these folks will take your bags and check them in. Your Mom or Dad will probably give them a few dollars to say thank you and make sure your bags make it to the right place.

Ticketing Staff: They will help you get your tickets, you can also check-in your bags with them if you didn't do that outside with the baggage clerk.

Gate Security: Before you can go to the gate, you have to go through security to make sure you don't have a porcupine in your bag. The Gate Security team helps you and your carry on bags go through the security check.

Gate Agent: This person will keep you updated on the status of your flight. If there are any delays they will let you know what time the plane will leave. When the plane is ready to board they will take your ticket and guide you to the plane.

Pilot/Co-Pilot: These are the men and women that will fly your plane.

Flight Attendant: The flight attendants sit in the cabin of the plane with the passengers. They will make sure you are safe and comfortable during your flight. If you have any questions, you can press the flight attendant call button above your seat and they will come to see you.

Glossary

Cockpit: The cockpit is like the driver's seat in a car. This is where the pilot and co-pilot control the plane from.

Control Tower: This is a tall building located at the airport. The pilots receive messages from the control tower telling them when to leave the gate, take off and land.

Flight Attendant: There will be one or more flight attendants in the cabin with you, they are there for your safety and comfort(in case you need a drink).

Gate: This is where the plane is parked to unload and load people (That's you!).

Jetway: This is a tunnel that connects the airport gate to the airplane so you can walk onto the plane without getting wet in the rain or cold in the winter.

Landing Gear: A plane usually has two sets of wheels under the wings and one wheel under the nose (front) of the plane. You will hear the gear fold up inside the plane after the plane takes off and you will hear it again when the pilot is getting ready to land.

Pilot: The pilot is part of the flight crew, the pilot is in charge of everything and everyone on the plane. There will be at least one co-pilot, and maybe more on larger planes. You will only see the pilot when you are getting on or off the plane, the rest of the time, the door to the cockpit will be closed.

Tarmac: This is the paved road the plane travels on when taking off and landing. The runway is the part of the tarmac that the plane uses to take off and land.

If you found this book of value, please consider <u>posting a review</u> on amazon. If you have any suggestions or comments I would love to hear from you, please email me kim.jenkins@stoneriversolutions.com.

Legal